To Jimmy Parker —

Who must have a good
bit of Indian blood to live
in Shawnee Mission! With
respect for his counsel, and
appreciation for his friendship —

6 November 75   Keith

John Groth

The Promise Kept

They made us many promises,
more than I can remember,
but they never kept but one;
they promised to take our land and they took it.
Sioux Indian to Reverend W. J. Cleveland

THE PROMISE KEPT

By Kurth Sprague Drawings by John Groth

1975   THE ENCINO PRESS   AUSTIN

This book is for
John Groth,
Artist and Friend
and for

Colonel James F. Hanger,
Anadarko, Oklahoma

&

Colonel Ray O. Embree,
Lawton, Oklahoma

And In Memory of
The Reverend Jesse Bushyhead,
Cherokee Baptist Minister
&
All Who Have Trod the Trail of Tears

Acknowledgments

I MAKE NO PRETENSE to being an historian—a confession which will, I am certain, gladden the hearts of those of my friends who essay the accompanying pages—and I would therefore be remiss as well as pretentious were I not to express my heartfelt gratitude toward those men and women who have helped me avoid errors in fact, as well as those who have aided me in evading the more egregious errors of literary correctness, this generous help enabling me to make less of an ass of myself than would have happened had I not had their welcome intervention: Roger Abrahams, Thomas M. Cranfill, Ambrose Gordon, Gerald Langford, Ruth P. M. Lehmann and W. P. Lehmann, and W. W. Newcomb, Jr., all of the University of Texas at Austin; Louis F. Bishop, III, and Chase Horton, of New York City; Sidney B. Brinckerhoff of the Arizona Historical Society; Dee Brown of the University of Illinois, Urbana, Illinois; Curator, Field Artillery Museum, Fort Sill, Oklahoma; T. R. Fehrenbach of San Antonio, Texas; Wayne Gard, of Dallas, Texas; Mrs. James F. Hanger, Anadarko, Oklahoma; Colonel Alfred R. Kitts, Army War College, Carlisle Barracks, Pennsylvania; F. J. Pearson, Jr., of Reston, Virginia; Mrs. Weckeah Bradley, grand-daughter of Quanah Parker, Lawton, Oklahoma; especially deserving of my appreciation is Robert M. Utley, Chief Historian of the National Park Service, whose books are superbly written, and a constant inspiration.

Finally, I thank my wife, Ruth McNamara Sprague, for the equanimity with which she endured the writing of this book, and the steadfast faith which she had in its eventual production.

Kurth Sprague

Austin, Texas

The only good Indians I ever saw were dead.
Philip Henry Sheridan, at Fort Cobb, Indian Territory, 1869.

What experience and history teach us is this—that
people and governments never have learned anything
from history, or acted on principles deduced from it.
Philosophy of History, Georg Wilhelm Friedrich Hegel.

Those who cannot profit by history are bound to repeat it.
Attributed to George Santayana.

Inasmuch as ye have done it unto one of the least of these
my brethren, ye have done it unto me.
Matthew 25:40.

It will be the same as last time; we will all die.
Russell Means, Wounded Knee, S.D., March 1973.

The Promise Kept

The Fort Sill Officers' Open Mess,
Saturday Nights, 1957

You'll REMEMBER there was the rumor of Suez that summer
And for us the very junior newly-commissioned
Second lieutenants, the uncertainty added
A spurious glamor and dignity.

On Saturday
Evenings we would all assemble in the great upstairs
Ballroom of the Officers' Club sitting at long tables
Silver-set and glass-laden and ranked around the dance floor.

It grew hot in that high hall, and someone would rise
And throw open one of the narrow casement windows
Letting in the wind from White Wolf Crossing,
From Mount Scott, Cache Creek,
Apache Crossing and Medicine Bluff.

Candles flickered when the winter wind
Came prowling, and a murmuring about Meissen
Was interrupted by a shiver, and a glance directed
At the open window where the wind intruded,
And a fur coat of "classic" cut
Might be thrown about bare shoulders.
Some officers wore dress blues, and their chests
Were bright with battle-ribbons and their brass
Was worn, and burnished to a winking white

Until the detail of infantry's crossed rifles,
Scabbard rings of cavalry's crossed sabres,
Or the touch-holes of artillery's crossed cannons
Had been obliterated by rouge and Blitz Cloth.
Compacts and cigarette cases littered the table;
Some were insignia-studded and showed the stars
Of famed generals, past posts served,
Far places and strange climes and distant times.
Across the table: eye glinting, bright lipstick and good teeth,
Faintly flushed the hectic cheek. Ah! Forget
The out-of-date dresses . . .

Song of the Officers' Wives

WE TRY to forget all our out-of-date dresses
With cocktails at sunrise and Officers' Messes:
Thirty years in the Army is just a fun spree
With infantry dog-robbers and dental work free!

We know we must answer to Washington's whim
Which doesn't deter us from odd bits of sin;
But firm in our minds is our husband's career:
We shall have Daiquiris; only soldiers drink beer!

Our choicest possessions are the Club and PX,
And target-cloth curtains and afternoon sex;
Why, perish the thought of a Reduction in Forces:
Give up the Bridge Club, and surrender the horses?

4

Oh, late in the evening when the last guest has gone
We shed tears in the wine and we sing a sad song,
We're wives in name only, and we fear what the wars
Might do to our army of misfits and bores!

So we try to forget all our out-of-date dresses,
With martinis at sunrise and officers' messes;
But we know we shall wait for that letter which comes
"We regret to inform you . . ." black crepe, and slow drums!

6

The Echoes Are Starting

THE ECHOES are starting which soon will awaken
Sleeping echoes of an age ago, lingering in the air
Longer than rare laughter, or slow weeping, or forsaken
Love its remembered glow. Up there
Hangs a battle-standard from a rafter:
Stained, faded, it is the tattered red-and-white
Of Grierson's Tenth Cavalry now, long after,
Famed for its fighting troopers once caught sight
Of by the Indians, and then forevermore
Known as "Buffalo Soldiers" for their woolly hair
And truculence like the buffalo in going to war
And standing up to Satanta, the White Bear
On Colonel Grierson's porch at old Fort Sill!
    "Right by fours!" apoplectic sergeants shout.

                              "Fours right into line!"
For hours they'd wheel and form and swoop in their drill!
Dressed right in straight line, under the sun how their brass
    did shine!

    Chivalry prompts me to mumble a fable
About its being warm, and I sign the bar-chit
And push back my chair, and get up from the table
And from the window I stare at the moon-lit
Landscape stretching featureless silver and sable.

Geronimo's Grave, East Firing Range

SAYING GOOD-NIGHT: wraps, coats, frosty breath,
"Drive carefully," "good-night," "good-night,"
And sometimes, later on, we'd drive out
On the East Firing Range
Down a yellow dirt road
In the wind and the moonlight
Where shadowed grass shook like a long surf
And willow trees swayed in the winter wind;
Down near the creek, rocks were necklaced by bear-claw ice.
On the radio, Music through the Night, and Carl Orff's
"O! Fortuna! Imperatrix!"
    I pull up the car, strip the seal and uncork the cognac;
With an easy effort, I swallow French fire eagerly.
"I don't know how you stand that stuff."
Far from the high hot hall, I look about.
    Between the road and the creek, in the rustling
Of the untended clumps and clusters of grass,
There shone in the moonlight of late winter,
Short white boards serried in the clay
Dressed and ranked like a task in survey,
The scudding clouds drifting aside
To show the ancient and precise array:
                    "Unknown Indian"
                    "Unknown Indian"
                    "Unknown Indian"
    In the midst of the markers, all the memorial you'll see
Behind a chain-link fence, high and stout,

Is a tall cairn of red stones, with a stone eagle on top:
"Geronimo."
Curiously, I thought, there was no desecration
Here, no beer cans, none of the detritus we leave behind
To make our mark. The Army kept it clean.
    They'll show you his cell at Sill, the stones worn down
In a circle where the Apache paced.
    " 'O, Fortune!' That's rather nice, isn't it?"
    "Yes, it is."
    Anyway, on Saturday nights late
I'd drive out to Geronimo's grave
On the East Firing Range, drink cognac and muse.

9

Wichita Mountain Wildlife Refuge

SUNDAY AFTERNOONS, top down, blast out that road
West toward Cache with the wind in your hair
And the sun in your eyes and a couple of cans
Of three-dismal-two! Pass by the old Blue Beaver
Then there'd be to your right the red rocky hills
And you'd turn in to the Wichita Wildlife Refuge,
And go slow.
　　　　Mad Bishop went out there a time or two with me.
Beer-drunk and broiling under the sun of an Oklahoma
Sunday, he'd dismount from the car like it was a Land Rover
And he was Francis Macomber, and then he'd take off
His Brooks Brothers blazer and now, looking like an Okie
Ordonez, he'd try to cape a buffalo bull.
　　　　　　　　　　　　　　　　Bishop was the one
Had Barnaby Conrad's cigarette case (so he said)
With the horn-gouge from "the old days in Madrid."
　　　　The buffalo stared at us dumbly. Phlegmatic,
Eyes red-rimmed, they ruminated patiently.
If we'd kept on with it, I'm sure they would have charged:
And no "line of duty" on *that* accident report!
　　　　The girls—satisfactorily—screamed at Bishop,
And then we'd go to picnic in the golden evening, under an oak,
And sometimes we'd catch a glimpse of brindled longhorn,
Or more buffalo, quite nearby, shaking the brush, ghosts from
　　　　　　　　　　　　　　　　the past.

The Translation of Quanah Parker,
Eagle of the Comanches,
Post Cemetery, Fort Sill, Oklahoma
9 August 1957

Resting here until day breaks,
and shadows fail, and darkness
disappears is Quanah Parker,
last chief of the Comanches.
       — Mrs. Neda Birdsong

1400 hours

THAT was the summer when the Army
At last acquired the land west of the post
Where Quanah Parker, the Eagle of the Comanches,
Was buried alongside his mother, Cynthia Ann.
They needed Post Oak Cemetery for part
Of a missile range; the new missile systems,
They said, demand more land:
So much was made manifest.

    Topay, Quanah's second wife, repudiated
By the remainder of his family
Since she'd remarried after the old chief's death,
Raised all kind of sand about that, loosing

Letters that flew like arrows, and firing off
Writs to be filed up there in Oke City
In District Court like there was no by-God tomorrow . . .
      It seemed remote from the raids and the roaming,
From where it all had taken place:
On the rocky naked plains, in the rock-strewn hills,
In the warm winds, in the zephyrs of springtime,
In the winds of the summer;
From the north, in the blue winds of autumn,
In the wild winds of white winter.
Where sun's blast blinds hunger's weak eyes,
Come then the voices of strength . . .
Comes then the strength of great medicine.
      The Army was trying to make it right,
So they were re-burying old Quanah, with his mother
Cynthia Ann, in the Fort Sill Cemetery;
And the honor guard, firing party, color guard
Were Amerindians serving in the Army,
Stationed at Fort Sill.
                              And great Quanah's

Giant grandsons carried the coffin,
Stepping carefully in store-bought shoes
Or bench-shaped boots; their bulk of shoulder
Straining the seams of their dark blue suits . . .
      Jesus!
      The grandsons of Quanah Parker were mighty men:
They had hands like freckled hams!
Flatfaced they were, and seeming impassive:
Well-guarded they held themselves against
Inevitable indignity; powerful, proud,
Their silver-belted bellies were huge,

12

Great-gutted and hard like a buffalo paunch,
Ballooning above their dainty feet
As if they'd rise effortless into the cloudless sky
And with great Quanah's coffin,
Float there above the grudging earth.
    In the bright sunshine, the ceremony
Achieved a sombre dignity,
Brilliantine lost its lustre
And the fire faded from where
The sunlight struck black hair.
The grandsons of Quanah Parker:
Henry, Wilbur, Elmer,
Charles, Leonard and Simmons Parker;
James and Ed Cox; Whit Choney;
Page Clifford, and Louis Clark.
    Under a canvas awning sat
Quanah's other kinfolk:
Old Baldwin Parker wept.
Tom and Len Parker, other sons,
Sat near him with their sisters
Neda Birdsong, Alice Purdy
and Wanda Page.
    Fort Sill's 77th Army band,
Under the direction of Chief Warrant Officer
H. W. Frost, began to play
Beethoven's funeral dirge.
And the All-Indian honor guard,
Commanded by Cherokee-Apache Master Sergeant
Donald R. Wilkerson, sprang to attention
And presented arms.
    Brass burned brightly like a raw flame,

Burnished by Brasso, by Blitz-Cloth
And rouge-rag. Sandblasted
Helmet-liners reflected light
Like quicksilver, while white-gloved hands
Slapped sling-loosened stocks
With a smart wallop! Shirts starched
Like sharp-edged boards,
Trousers bloused wrinkleless
And weighted by chains taped
To Number Ten tin cans.
    Now the band was quiet,
And Major General Thomas E. DeShazo,
Commanding General, U.S. Army Artillery
And Missile Center, got up to speak.
We saw the general wore the summer uniform
Of short-sleeved shirt and shorts.
We were all quiet, and he began his speech:
"Quanah continually inspired his people
To greater efforts in taking up the new way
Of life, in learning how to plow . . ."
    I thought then of another time,
Of another general, dressed in civilian clothes
Stalking a porch at Sill . . .

14

Headquarters, Fort Sill,
Indian Territory,
Department of the Missouri,
27 May 1871

General of the Army
William Tecumseh Sherman
("The Great Warrior").

AGENT Lawrie Tatum's letter
Lay between Grierson and me
Out of the way of the chessboard.
Grierson broke the silence:
"You say it was Mamanti, The Sky-Walker,
The medicine man, who led this raid?"
        "That's my suspicion. But it was Satanta
That told me, bragging, how it was at Salt Creek.
Then asking for rifles and ammunition—
Satanta, the White Bear,
The one with the big mouth,
He's the one for some reason
Wants to take credit for it.
That's why I sent thee that letter."
        We stared at him.

"I guess thee might say," Tatum told us,
"My pacifist tendencies are bankrupt."
        Grierson and I could understand a man like that.
        Grierson spoke lightly. "He just came in
And told you all that?"
        "Just so," said Bald Head Tatum.
"Right here in the 'City of Refuge'."
        "What kind of man is he?" I asked,
Looking at the chessboard, all black and white,
Like the western plains when the sun
Bleaches all color to a monochrome.
        "Satanta, does thee mean? Or them others?
Big Tree, Kicking Bird, Satank or Lone Wolf?"
        "I meant Satanta. White Bear."
        "Were I you, General," Grierson said,
"I wouldn't entirely neglect old Satank."
        "The old one who lost his son."
        "Raiding in Texas. Yes. That's the one.
Carries the boy's bones with him, he does,
On a pony. Everywhere. Sets up a platform
Every night, puts out food and drink."
        "Well," said Bald Head, "Satanta
Is a big burly one for'n Indian.
Wears an officer's blouse;
Sometimes he blows a bugle."
        "Marcy can tell you," I said. "We heard
A bugle that day in the Daugherty wagon
When we crossed Salt Creek."
        "They plumb passed thee by," Bald Head
Said. "Thee has old Mamanti the Sky Walker
To thank for that. They waited till thee was gone,

Waited for that wagon train of Warren's."
        "General," said the adjutant
Stepping into the room,
Ignoring the chessboard,
"General, he's come."
        Grierson peered out
Between the closed shutters.
"My God, he's got a bugle."
        Yes, I nodded.
        "Why you reckon, General,
Those Indians passed you by?"
        "Maybe they liked my nice
Indian middle name."
        "Tecumseh was a prophet,"
Bald Head Tatum said, sounding amused.
        I passed through the orderly room
Crammed solid with sweating black troopers
Of Grierson's Tenth. In chess,
There were just the black and white.
Washington and the War Department
Had refined the game, I thought:
Now we had red.
        All wars were mad.
        I stepped onto the porch;
My sense of absurdity grew:
While I exercised a general's whim
And wore civilian clothes,
Satanta, under a blanket in the broiling heat,
Was wearing a captain's coat
Cadged from God only knew whose corpse.
At his side hung the bugle.

Maybe the grease kept flies away,
I thought, looking at where the braids had rubbed
Against the collar of his coat,

                                and then,

Not willing it, I took his hand in mine,
And I must have smiled,
And though he could not know it,
The smile was not for him:
Quick to see a thousand slights,
Custer refused that red hand
Two years before.
What matter of it if Satanta and I
Understood each other?
That's no deterrent to a fight.
Why, regard our but-lately-concluded
Fratricide: both Federal and Confederate
Understood each other as befits brothers!
Recall the nomenclature of a conflict:
A 'battle' is what the war's winner calls it;
But if the war's winner
Suffer annihilation in a skirmish,
That's a 'massacre'.
        Our eyes were speaking truth,
While our tongues were telling lies.
        Behind me I could sense Grierson's blacks
And in the distance I could hear
A muffled curse and a cough from the cavalry
Kept waiting my word in the stone corral.
        "Ho. Great Warrior."
        "Ho. Satanta. White Bear."
        I dropped his hand,

And once more we were formal and ritual.
Satanta started to say something,
And I thought he was going to stroke my arm
And blurt out like Walking Bird did Custer,
"You heap nice sonabitch, you big sonabitch."
But Satanta did no such thing,
And the moment passed.

   "Ho, Great Warrior: I, Satanta, White Bear,
With my men took many wagons, many mules
Down in Texas raiding. . . ."

   Satanta had the words just right,
Rippling from his tongue.

   I, too, knew from old,
The words which must be said: "All right, Satanta,
You have admitted this bad thing in front of all,
And so I order your arrest with Big Tree
And Satank to stand trial in Texas."

   Big Tree is not here, Satanta told me.

   No matter, I told Satanta. We will wait.
We will find him. You can count on that.

   What about Kicking Bird, Satanta
Wanted to know.

   Kicking Bird tried to make you walk
In the paths of peace, I told him. Kicking Bird
Goes free.

   Satanta looked away from me.
"The corn you give me makes my gums to bleed,"
He complained. "Long ago, we are hunters,
Then we learn, we teach ourselves
To hunt the buffalo, otherwise we die.
Now not very many buffalo. All gone,
You wasting all meat.
And you teach us plant corn.
You all crazy. The white men crazy.
No goddamned good." And he spat on the porch.

   "Very well," I said. "You will remain here
With—"

   Satanta shrugged, and lifted from beneath
His blanket a revolver hidden there.
Kicking Bird, from among the milling crowd
Below, held up a rifle high, and yelled
Out clear, "You and I will die right here!"

   I raised my arm then,
And behind my back the shutters burst open
Slamming against the stone with hellish force.
Breasting the windows were the black troopers
Of the Tenth, the "buffalo soldiers",
Bristling with carbine barrels like a swarm
Of buzzing bluebottles. And from the stone corral
Where they'd been waiting sweating in the sun,
Came trotting a column of cavalry,
"Squads left into line . . . *ho*!
Tro-o-o-p . . . *halt*!"

   I had little trouble after that,
After white, the color of no color,
Disengaged, and left black facing red.

17

On the Fort Richardson Road,
8 June 1871

George Washington,
Chief of the Caddoes
("Caddo George"):

THEY SAY I sell guns and liquor to the Caddo people.
I look after my people. That is the God's truth.
I have a thing I must tell you about what happened
On the Fort Richardson road.
They all knew me at Fort Sill in those days.
They all knew Caddo George.
Lieutenant Thompson's men took Satank,
Satanta and Big Tree out from the little room
At the jail, and the three of them stood there
And they all had heavy iron on their hands and legs,
And the sun was hurting their eyes bad.
Satank, he have a knife, he kept it hidden.
He go to shake hands with Grierson
And then he try to stab him with the knife.
Satanta and Big Tree, they pull him back.
Satanta and Big Tree, they both real quiet,
And they not fight when the soldiers push them
Up in the wagons. But old Satank, he not move
When soldiers come round to him. He just stand there,

20

Real small with long gray hairs on his lip
Like an old yellowskin, standing there by himself in the sun.
    Then Lieutenant Thompson, he get mad,
He tell soldiers what to do
And then they take old Satank
He don't weigh much they throw him
Up into wagon. Satank, he in first wagon,
The others Big Tree and Satanta they in second.
All still handcuff, and chain, hands and legs.
By-and-by Lieutenant Thompson,
He say to Mackenzie Lieutenant, he name Thurston,
"It is done. Now it is yours." And he smile.
They wave at each other like soldiers,
And then we leave Fort Sill.
Then Satank he sit up in the corn
Wagon full of, and he start to make a song.
He sing how he belong Ko-eet-senko,
With Kiowas only ten men belong Ko-eet-senko,
That warrior group only brave men.
When young, Satank say he come back
Always with honor. Now he say he like dog,
He cannot come back with honor now.
Satank's son the one he die in Texas
Long time Satank carry bones with him everywhere,
Those bones back at Fort Sill now, so Satank
Say he want to die now, be with his son.
This is song old Satank sing:
    "O sun, you stay always,
    But we Ko-eet-senko die now,
    O land, you stay always,
    But we Ko-eet-senko die."

The Man Who Knows All Words, Jones,
He tell two-stripes ride near me
That Satank he ready to do something bad.

Brevet Major General Benjamin H. Grierson,
Colonel Commanding Tenth United States Cavalry;
Post Commander, Fort Sill, Indian Territory:

Mackenzie had stayed behind
To have a few words with me
After the wagons and guard had gone.
He was still extremely fatigued
From his exertions in the field.
General Sherman had sent him in pursuit
Of the perpetrators of the Warren massacre
At Salt Creek Prairie, and he'd left
Fort Richardson on nineteen May,
Remaining in the field until four June
When he arrived at Fort Sill only to find
That the three chiefs were in chains,
Ready to return to Texas and stand trial.
    Mackenzie and I were talking,
The guard and the wagons
Had gone over the hill.
There was an unmelodic humming noise
That must have come from old Satank
Carried on the hot still air.
You could hear this unharmonic
Lament all over the post,
They said later on.

Then there were several shots
Coming close together,
And then there was a moment's silence,
And then there was a long-drawn-out
Ragged volley that went on and on.
Upon the first shots being fired,
Colonel Mackenzie mounted his horse
And set off at a brisk trot in the direction of his command.

Caddo George:

Old Satank, he speak to me in Comanche,
He tell me stealing mules was wrong,
And his people got to do what Bald Head Tatum say.
Then Satank tell me he die along this road,
That his people come after he dead
And pick up all his bones.
Then Satank begin singing again,
And then the soldiers make fun
The way old Satank sing, and they try
To sing like Satank sing. But old Satank,
He make Ko-eet-senko death song, and the soldiers,
They make song about a brush-hen in the bushes.
Then he ask me do I see big pecan tree alongside road.
That when his wagon reach that tree, Satank die.
I holding then the silver cross
White Man Who Wear Black Dress has given me,
And then I think may be my pony has stepped on stone,
And I get off pony and pick up his foot
Looking for stone there, until wagon gone by and Satank,

He coming up to pecan tree,
And I look round me at soldiers smiling,
Making song about bird in bushes,
But Satanta and Big Tree, they hear Satank
All right, they look like they dead theirselfs
Sitting there in second wagon.
Then Satank, he tell Tonk scout,
He can have scalp, and Tonk squaw scream loud.
Then I very scared and let soldiers go by me.

Lieutenant George K. Thurston,
Fourth United States Cavalry:

I was Officer of the Day.
I placed two armed guards in each wagon.
The two drivers were civilian, and they rode the near wheelers.
I rode next to the second wagon;
The remainder of my company rode behind me.
The road was very narrow.
For that reason neither I nor any of my men
In the company following
Could clearly see the action in the first wagon.
At first, there was only the noise
From the old man's singing.
Then some members of my command, I regret to say,
To break the boredom, were aping
His caterwauling, and mocking him.
But the old Indian's singing stopped
When the first wagon drew abreast
Of the big pecan tree by the side of the road.

23

24

At once then, there was a commotion,
And I reined out to the side of the road
To get a better view.
Satank took hold of his guard's carbine,
And was trying to wrest it from the soldier's grasp.
    Old Satank was quick,
And he must have been strong as well,
For almost immediately the struggle had ended
With the guard being tossed out of the wagon,
And the Indian keeping the carbine.
Satank sprang the lever prior to firing,
And, "expecting every instant to see him
Succeed in the attempt, I concluded
That the Indian had better die, and right speedily,
And I gave the command to fire"

Corporal Joseph H. Robinson,
Company D, Fourth United States Cavalry:

I have followed the guidon for fourteen years.
I served right through the War of the Rebellion.
I have been a sergeant twice;
Each time, due to some trouble not of my making,
I lost my stripes.
I have not had a drink in over three months.
I was part of Colonel Mackenzie's command
That pursued Satanta and Big Tree and them,
From after the Warren Massacre at Salt Creek
All the way to Fort Sill. In the field, we were,
Over two weeks, leaving Fort Richardson

25

In the driving rain. My horse went lame,
And so Lieutenant Thurston assigned me
To ride in the first wagon with the old red nigger.
I beg pardon, sir, I mean the old Indian.
	The old Indian, he started singing
When we was leaving Fort Sill,
And he kept it up after we left.
He said something to Caddo George
And then he said something to the Tonk
Scout and his woman, and then *she*
Made a loud noise, too.
My head hurt along with my stomach.
My stomach been hurting me ever since
We left Fort Richardson, and I went
To the doctor when I got back.
All of a sudden, the nig-
I mean, the old Indian,
Somehow had got his hands free,
And was wrestling my carbine away from me,
And before I knew it,
He'd thrown me out of the wagon.
As I fell, he stabbed me with a second knife
He'd had hidden. After that,
He started to raise my carbine.
I saw his hands and wrists then.
They was all bloody like raw meat
And they was strips hanging from them
Where the handcuffs had been.
I heard the lieutenant give
The command to fire,
And after the first shots he went down,

But I wasn't surprised to see him
Get back on his feet again.
The men kept on firing then,
Some of them reloading their weapons
And emptying them again.
It took the old Indian a long
Time to die, and by that time,
Colonel Mackenzie had caught up with us
And he told us to unload the body
And put it side of the road,
And then we rode on by,
The whole troop of us, and the two
Other Indians in the other wagon,
On our way back to Fort Richardson.
The Tonk scout took his scalp.
Now I am waiting on my discharge papers.
I have a sister in Paterson, New Jersey,
Where I am going to live.
I still have twinges in my leg,
I told the doctor, where
The old red nigger stabbed me.

Brevet Major General Ranald Slidell Mackenzie,
Colonel Commanding Fourth United States Cavalry,
Fort Richardson, Texas:

When I arrived at Fort Sill
After having been in the field
For fourteen days, I was surprised
To find the Indians under guard there.

On the afternoon of eight June
We were leaving Fort Sill
With the three Indians.
I stayed behind in the adjutant's office,
Talking with Grierson, and I suppose
I must have been aware that one of the Indians,
Old Satank, was making a noise,
But it is my understanding that, for an Indian,
This kind of noise is not unusual.
As I was talking with Colonel Grierson,
There came two volleys of shots
Some moments apart,
And I immediately mounted and rode
To where I found the old Indian,
Satank, down in the loose corn of the wagon-bed,
Crawling and coiling like a crippled serpent,
Covered with blood.
　　　Reconstructing the event,
What had happened was this:
Satank had concealed a second knife
Upon his person,
And he had stabbed his guard,
A booze-ridden corporal named Robinson,
And then wrested his carbine from him.
At this point, young Thurston
Had given the command for the column
To open fire, fearing further injury.
But the doughty Indian,
Like many of his species
A durable specimen,
Got to his feet again, although

From the blood which poured from his mouth
He had been pierced through the lungs
And it was only a matter of time until
He should have expired, wounded, as he was,
Mortally. But there was life,
And the will to kill in him yet,
And, whether acting from humanitarian impulses
In concert with a divine Providence,
Or in protection of his own command,
Thurston quite correctly gave the command to fire
Again, at will, and this the men did,
Until their weapons were empty.
Some, perhaps taking out upon the hapless Indian
Their wrath and frustration for the past weeks
Of fruitless and exhausting pursuit about the desert
Fired and reloaded their weapons, firing again,
And emptying them again.
　　　At last, I could clearly see the old man
Was close to death, and though I felt it
A healthy sign that the men had some physical object
On which to vent their rage,
With reluctance, but with knowledge
That this was my Christian duty,
I forbore the men to fire again,
And called them from their quarry.
I have put all these events in my report.
I have commended the prompt action
Of Lieutenant Thurston, and have seen to it
That Robinson, the guard, be discharged
From the service without prejudice.

Caddo George:

The last thing I remember
Is old Satank
Sitting there in the dust
Leaning back against the tree
With the blood from his mouth.

The Translation of Quanah Parker,
Eagle of the Comanches,
Post Cemetery, Fort Sill, Oklahoma
9 August 1957
1425 hours
Conclusion

THE funeral speech was ending;
The sun was lower in the sky.
Cashmere Bouquet's wedding with Old Spice
Hung heavy on the heated air,
A sop to decency, sweat's sacrifice.
Cynthia Ann Parker, Quanah's mother,
The general said—predictably—
Was "a shining example of motherhood."

    It was hot as hell, and all the Indians
In and out of uniform were as wilted
As the rest of us, and more bored.
Past resentment, anyway; past almost
Anything you could think of,
Except, perhaps, a kind of numb amusement
In wondering what else might now be turning up
In this transitory life while the shadows lengthen,
Out of the sly white trickster's bag of tricks.
    Bishop nudged me. "Cynthia Ann," he mused,

"God, doesn't it sound like Grace Kelly, though?"
And he peered round, inspecting,
To detect resemblance.
    We detected none.
    "I wonder what she thought
When she saw those Rangers come?"
    "No, it was MP's," I said,
"Not Rangers went for Topay."
    "Not Topay; his old lady, the one's
'A shining example of motherhood.' "
    Somebody turned around to shush us.
    Colonel Lexington Sheffield,
The Post Chaplain now ratified the general's remarks,
And then Quanah Parker's great-grand-daughter,
Cynthia Ann Bradley, came forward and laid
Yellow gladiolas on great Quanah's grave.
    The firing party, commanded by
Cherokee Sergeant First Class Woodrow Scott,
Cracked out three volleys, practised,
In commendable unison—order—*Ker-blam!*
Reply. *Ker-blam!* Reply. *Ker-blam!*
Reply! And the white-haired General gently
Gave the folded flag to Wanda Page,
Quanah's eldest present child, just as
Taps was sounded, live and quavering on the air,
Very sad, like an evening dress put on in afternoon.
    We tried to leave then to beat the rush
To the club, take the rest of the afternoon off,
Get a drink in the cool.
    Behind us, the band, with irony
Unconscious and sweet struck up "Hail to the Chief!"

29

Santa Fe, New Mexico, 1960

"OLD MAN," I said, "how long you been sitting here?"

It was dusty and dirty, this stinking town,
And I was waiting for a bus.

He shrugged.

"Old man," I said, "whyn't you look around you,
                                    tell me what you see . . ."

And, for a moment, mirth welled in the mild blue
Of his cataract-frosted eyes.

Then I looked around me, feeling the hot still day
Alive, but barely so, by afternoon expiring,
Having hung crucified on the shaft of sundrenched morning
Pouring down desert air thick and bright and brittle
                                    as crystal:

Peeling chrome car lots were there, and sad cafes
Where music wailed moaning, sometimes heard
Gunshot-curt between bursts of brilliant silence
As glass doors pressed shut against refrigerated air.

After sunset, the heavy-faced whores would walk, promenading
In the heliotrope dusk, high-heeled
On hard sidewalks where pomaded youths lounged

Cock-proud and cash-poor, preening themselves
Like peacocks, or like glossy otters slick from a waterfall.

Above and beyond us, rimming the ridge of the blue
                                        desert and hills,
Was the circle of scarlet where the sun sank low.

"Not much like the old days, I guess," I said. "Well, here
Chief . . ." I dropped a quarter in his cup.
"Don't drink too much firewater."

My bus was in.

Song of the Old Man

The unseen sun's warmth but not its light
Burns now into my blind eyes,
Strong as my childhood and youth
And I am not now old, but only alone,
And the voices I hear are no longer those of even my children,
And the voices I hear are the voices of strangers.

Why do I not grow old?

Time's past is like a leaf's mold long rotten now,
But having known the earth's green veiling,
The summer heat, the lightening, the ripening

31

32

Yielding to a shimmering change of leaf-gold in autumn
And then a shroud of snow and the sickness of the
                                    death-wind blowing.

Time past is a skull-tree, black in the blue-stone sky
With a bloody sun behind black bird-flutterings,
And dry bones in a high-hung buffalo robe
With jar and lance and dead pony beneath,
While the wind sweeps the skull-tree's branches
Lightly at night, and the rotting,
The quiet bird-fluttering foulness,
Has homed to the ochre-bright moon.

                         So long ago, the steel-hats came,
Trod beast-black with beard, and the hooves of their bodies
Churned the earth to dust.
                         And they carried blossoming death
In their red-flower hands,
And they brought disease to our women, and disgrace to our lodges.

    The steel-hats came from the southland, and their very speech
Sounded a deathrattle, but we were poor,
And they left the flat land,
But some gazed up as though moonstruck among sand and rock,
Eyeless they gazed to the black cloak above,
And the dry feathers shivered
In a crack of moon-blue steel.

    This was in the late summer of our world.

33

The Trail of Tears
1838
Near Hopkinsville, Kentucky.

The Reverend Jesse Bushyhead:

I

*I*N *the Name of God, Amen!*
O, Lord, who hast promised
            that when two or three of us
Are gathered together, Thou wilt
            hear our prayer . . .
        I, thine unworthy servant, Jesse,
Must have speech with Thee!
        Here, O Lord, is a sight to break the hardest heart,
Melt like a morning's dew the adamantine soul:
Waggons, oxen, horses, children, men and women—
All our woeful train is now winding westward
Like some primordial serpent slithering
Along the muddy path. An utter desolation of the soul
Does greet Thee, from men and women infirm with age,
And others inconsolable, though not yet past their innocence.
                                    The weight
Of rain bends down the broad-leaved trees

Jesse Bushyhead
from portrait
by C. B. King

35

And the doleful entourage plods onward
And we trudge along the trail through twilight glades
Toiling toward an illusory Jordan.
The raucous plumage of a bird, bright in this miasmic
Gloom, appearing somehow absurd, is denied
The uplifting glance of a single sullen eye;
Bubbles of fetid mud release their stench
While we cover over children in unmarked roadside graves
And then *press on, press on!* The faces of our guards
Are not pitiless, but only powerless to assist.
 In the evenings beside the stagnant waters,
Our voices raise old songs in dark groves;
In the evenings beside the fever-haunted waters
Where the willows grow:

 Our seed shall sojourn in the land a stranger.
  O, Lord, speak to us in the visions of the night.
 Our lives are forfeit, our souls in danger.
  Speak to us, O Lord, and make the darkness light.
 Our flight is not famine-forced, and we fear to go.
  O, Lord, out of the bondage of Egypt, deliver us.
 Make us flee not our Canaan, nor old Jordan's flow.
  Deliver us, O Lord, from Egypt, keep us from
       the wilderness.
 The wilderness has shut us in, we are entangled in the land.
  O, Lord, we should be as sheep in the midst of wolves.
 Lovely Canaan lies behind us, ahead lifts Pharoah's wicked hand.
  Let thy stiff-necked people, O Lord, be wise as
       serpents and gentle as doves!

 The song is ended, and the only sound

Is one of our women weeping, salting the sodden trail,
Wet already, with her widow's tears.

II

The day had been sultry and there was a storm that afternoon
And from the side of the road where I'd been resting
I saw a fine bay horse and a buggy burdened down
And all bedraggled, passing by.
Just as they came up to me, there was a lightning flash:
The frightened horse hock-deep in mud,
The reluctant buggy loaded down with belongings,
And the occupants (husband, wife and small child),
Were all in that instant etched in my mind as if by acid.
    The husband had the lofty forehead and the imperious eye
That are the unconscious accoutrements of station;
But the pinched white nostril in the high-colored face
Betokened disaster in some desperate enterprise.
You could tell his mouth was used to smiling
But it was bitter and down-twisted now,
And his careful suit and high-wound stock were drenched:
Fear reached out from this man like a sudden stench.
"Our farm . . . my horses . . . Paris dresses . . ."
    His wife sat next to him on the narrow seat.
She was leaning forward, attempting to protect
The infant in her arms against the elements.
Her streaming hair was all disordered, loose and disarranged,
And neglect gave up to nature once again her raven tresses;
Her eyes glittered like the chips of jet
That a patient seamstress had sewn upon her dress.

37

You could feel this woman's fury, implacable, savage, wild:
Cold and black like the ice of winter was her rage.
    The only note of warmth in this whole chill scene
Came from the dim faint fire on her fingers
Of ruby and amethyst. Her dress was right, too,
I saw, for Rachel: black silk bombazine.
"Our farm . . . his horses . . . my Paris dresses. . . ."
    They drove on.
    Soon I knew, that wavering wheel would fall.
    Soon the horse would pull up lame, and girth-galled.
    The child was dead already, I could tell.
"Their farm . . . his horses . . . her Paris dresses . . ."

III

O, Lord! O, Holy Father! Please hear my prayer!
Here are my sweet people being torn from their homeland.
Our fathers before us were born in that land
And we were ourselves blessed who were born there.
It was like a garden, like Eden before the Fall,
And there, by increase of families and flocks
You made our people to prosper mightily;
Skills and science and crafts and trades you taught us,
You gave us government after the whiteman's way;
Like him, we had schools, we built roads, published
Newspapers, even traded and travelled across the sea.
And we had loved our good homeland:
The deep valleys and the rounded hills,
The dark valleys and mountains;
The great rivers and the mossy rocks,

38

The green rivers and boulders;
The torrents of the cataracts,
The foaming white torrents of waters;
The tall steepled trees,
The bark-lichened birches;
The morning mists over the water,
Over blue water stole the gold mists of morning;
The lakes, the sunsilvered creeks,
Brooks, glades, meadows, fields,
And the green valleys and the mountains the color of smoke.
This is the land we had taken and loved,
Settled and farmed it
And given to God. *Blessed be the Name of the Lord!*
    Now, in the space of a young man's lifetime,
We have become suddenly as calves in the land of the wolf;
Our homes and farms are seized, our livelihood
Cut off, and we are expelled from the garden
Our poor paradise, and we are scourged, and we flee
From Eden, from the forests and glades of our beloved land.
Now it is late autumn, and in the wet weather
Our fields, derelict, will have fallen fallow.
Harried are we from our homeland,
And on our hearths, the firecoals have faded
To embers, cooled down to ashes,
As we are driven now to the broken land, the rocky land,
And through this wilderness on our way west
To Egypt, waits death on every hand.

O Lord, deliver us!

39

IV

O, Lord! I know that I cannot
Catch Leviathan with a fish-hook,
Nor can I bind his tongue with a cord!
I seek no solace for myself,
Even as I give succour to the sick,
For I know that it is not right that I should seek a sign,
Some pillar of cloud by day or fire by night,
Perhaps, to mark our way through wilderness.

The time is not yet right, we have not yet
Reached Egypt; our time of testing is far off;
We must yet endure a bitter bondage
Before we are set free and see Thy Son!
Alleluia! In the Name of the Lord, Alleluia!
We travel toward the setting sun
And our way now leads through wilderness,
Our spirits are o'erwhelmed by weariness,
Our cheeks now wet with weeping,
With lamentations and loud cries,

Mourners made fast by bonds of mud
While our children die at every mile.
Yea, though I walk, Lord, yea, though I walk,
I yet need fear no one! Yea, though I walk, Lord,
Though I am led to bondage, Lord,
And the time of testing not begun,
I shall fear no evil, Lord, for I shall
Keep the faith and wait the coming of your Son.

In the Name of the Lord, Alleluia!

44

Song of the Buffalo

We faced each other in the night, before the fire,
And the first man had a head like unto a lion,
And the second unto a calf, and the third like unto a bear,
And the fourth man had a head like unto an eagle.
And we were painted men.
　　Thou wert our protector, thou wert our life;
Thee did we worship.
Thou took us through valley and stream and mountain
And desert places.
Thy body and thy bones kept us, and gave us life;
Thou wert feast in a land of famine,
And gave us great joy about the evening fires.
Then did thy happiness follow the hunter,
And when we died, it was thy cloak that covered us,
Protected us against the cold,
When we hung in a skull black tree.
　　Thou delivered us from sickness and pestilence;
Thou covered us and anointed us, afforded us implement,
And the dry dung of thy bowels burned brightly
So that we feared not any terror by night
Nor did any plague come nigh our tepee;
Thou gave us clothing and armor
Against the rain and bruising rock
And shield against our adversaries.
　　Therefore, we set thee on high, and worshipped thee,
And fell down and called to thee and made sacrifice
In the wilderness for thy bounty.

45

Hunter and hunted—*together*!
Clad in wolf-skins, sometimes our youths
Would stampede thee over cliff-side
In a brown falling torrent with the dust
And the tumult, and broken bodies below:
Ribs for the fletchers; tongue, and liver
For the brave young hunters,
And a feast of hump-meat and marrow-butter;
Hides for the women; bones for needles and awls . . .
    For we were given the running
Of the hot blood from thy life-flank
When we ran with thee: leg locked about
Pony barrel sometimes so close in the running
Our leg bone bumping buffalo shoulder
Feeling between horse hide and rough robe both hearts beating:
Hunter and hunted—*together*!
    The hot blood from thy pierced flank
Sped down thy side. Women came keening then,
With knives and bowls, almost before heart-beat
Had fled, and our men clustered about thee
In the throes of thy dying, and the blood
From thy body created in our old men and children
A wonderful strength.
    For this there was singing, life renewed
In our lodges. Here was food and shelter and clothing
And the warmth of fire thou gave us from the filth
                                    of thy bowels
Dried in the sun upon the prairie.
Yay, even thy heart's jailhouse endured in minute manner:
Every bone had a purpose.

46

48

The Ballad of a Buffalo Hunter, William H. McLean
1872–1883

IN HARTFORD, I worked as a street-car conductor,
A-punching your tickets and taking your fare;
And one day I did spy me a young Boston lassie
With blue in her eyes and bows in her hair.

Oh, she waxed most indignant and thoroughly angry
When I asked her to marry and share in my life;
"Oh, sir," said she, "but your prospects are fearful,
You have not the wealth to provide for your wife."

So Hartford I left then to join with my brother,
I went West to old Wayne in Seventy-Two;
I went for a-looking to sport me some buffalo,
I went for a-looking to run buffalo.

Oh, one day I left me old Hartford by railroad,
A steam locomotive did take me out West;
I travelled to Kansas by Santa Fe Railway,
And at old Dodge City I finally took rest.

It happened that evening that I went a-walking,
A-walking and searching for my brother Wayne;
I asked at "Dog" Kelly's, and then at Charles Rath's,
My brother's location to tell and explain.

Mister Rath, he done told me that Wayne had been selling
Some tongues to the Cox House for travellers to eat;
Now his wagon he drove out to camp on the prairie,
But soon he'd return for to sell more fresh meat.

Old Wayne, he did show up a-pulling his wagon
To Lobenstein's hide-house on that very day;
Then a clerk, he did yell out, "McLean better watch out,
Here's a Hartford policeman come to take him away!"

Oh, we set out next morning to find me an outfit;
We set out next morning to find me some guns:
An eleven-pound Sharps and a Navy revolver,
A case of good knives and six bottles of rum.

To Kiowa Creek we went then a-riding,
And passed the evening in sleeping on ground.
We made up our bedrolls, and when the dawn came,
We suddenly noticed there's snow all around.

Wayne, he did tell me before the campfire,
"If it should happen you do see a stand,
Pass up the heart shot, and try for the lungs, boy,
The trick is to keep them in one milling band."

That was the winter we stayed near Dodge City,
That was the winter that many men died;
They was frozen to death then, all out on the prairie,
And the buffalo hunters were last rites denied!

But we wintered good then, the hunting was good then,
We killed many buffalo, and shipped many hides;
The first month we shot and we killed and we shipped them,
Of pounds, twenty thousand, and of hides three-oh-five.

We shot then the shaggies all through the cold winter
Aiming first for the lungs and then for the heart;
They'd drop to their knees then, and give a great beller,
They'd snort and they'd snuffle, and rip a loud fart.

Oh, the stink and the stench of the shaggies they cured me
From ever becoming a skinner for sure;
The ticks and the lice and the graybacks they bit me—
And the romance of hunting had lost its allure!

Oh, from my head's top to the sole of my foot,
I looked like a blister or ambling sore:
Like a henchman of hades I worked a sharp knife,
At sundown too tuckered to wash off the gore.

I fell asleep then all covered with blood,
Burnt red from the sun and with nicks on my hands;
The grime and the dirt and the dung they did coat me—
I looked like a ghost out a-walking this land!

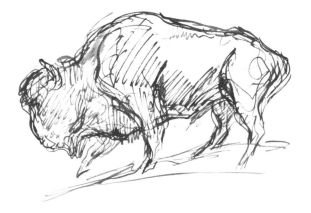

I dreamed I was browsing all over the prairie
And bowing my bearded head down real low;
I dreamed then I bellered and snorted and snuffled;
I dreamed I'd become just a real buffalo!

One day from my work I did glance up and look at

The mountains and plains which encircled me 'round:
The buffalo, they glittered like glass in a window,
Skint carcasses shining in one great big mound.

Oh, they looked like they fell then like manna from heaven,
But they was the fruit that the Grim Reaper gleaned:
They was scattered all over like leaves in a clearing,
But next year come Spring, they would not turn up green!

The next year we hunted all over the prairie,
From the Platte in the North through the country down South,
And the buffalo, they ran in the hundreds of millions:
We shot and they staggered with blood from their mouth!

Our needle guns booming, we shot shaggies by thousands—
We'd shoot 'em till our barrels grew certainly hot—
Then we'd put aside one gun, and reach for another,
When water was scarce, why, we'd piss down the spout!

One day in the winter, when Wayne went out hunting,
He got lost in a blizzard and he could not see;
His hands and his feet were all numb from the frost-bite,
His face was half-frozen and he'd bloodied a knee.

Then he found him a buffalo, and shot him and skinned him,
And wrapped himself up in the shaggy's warm hide;
He woke up to find out that he could not move then—
The hide was froze solid and Wayne was inside!

Oh, he could hear wolves that were snapping and yowling;
Why, their teeth were clipping right next to his ears—

So, he cussed them and hollered all through the cold night-time—
He yelled and he hollered to lessen his fears!

Next morning at sunrise, old Wayne was plumb tuckered
From cussing and swearing all through the long night,
But the sun when it came up did start to unthaw him,
When he got back to camp, why his hair done turned white!

Oh, Wayne, he would sit then before the campfire,
A-mumbling and cursing all under his breath:
He sat there a-staring; his face was a-twitching—
But he'd been saved from a fate worse than death!

Oh, it came the midnight and I did wake up
And see old Wayne with a gun in his hand:
He'd heard in the distance a branch that was breaking,
But there wasn't a soul in this empty land!

His face was all yellow and kind of decrepit,
And his eyes was like pitch-holes and burning real bright,
And his lips they had pulled back and showed his teeth snarling—
Like the Father of Sin, Wayne was sure a poor sight!

Oh, I talked to him gentle and quiet and soft then,
And the gun I did take from his trembling hand.
I made him sit down then, and have some hot soup then,
But by noon Wayne was back shooting buffalo stands!

Now the herds they was thinning, and moving away some
From the Platte in the North to the Cimarron;
They said that to Texas was where they had gone,

Plenty hunting in Texas where the slaughter went on!

That June we was camped at the Walls called Adobe,
When we went down to Texas in Seventy-Four:
There we did meet then a good many hunters
Who threw down their bedrolls on Hanrahan's floor.

A couple of soldiers and Chapman the scout had
A mysterious message to give to the Walls;
They talked then real quiet to some of the hunters
And when midnight came, they did open the ball!

"The ridgepole is breaking," yells out the bartender,
"Get up men, we're suffering an Indian attack!
It's Chief Quanah Parker has now come a-calling,
Come to pay his respects with a Comanche bush-whack!"

Now did the hunters all wake and start looking,
They thought that the store was a-tumbling down:
Some was still drunk and asleep and a-cursing
Old Quanah Parker a-coming to town!

Oh, Hanrahan heard then amid the great racket
The cry of Bill Dixon, who gave a loud shout,
"Good Godalmighty, it's redskins all-righty;
Boys, shoot with your rifles and let them ring out!"

So we sat up and listened to Hanrahan's orders
Drunk and half-dressed as some of us was;
We stumbled and fumbled our trousers to step in,
We picked up our pieces, and soon the place buzzed!

Well, it turned out much later that Chapman, he knew
That June Twenty-Seventh was that very date
When Chief Quanah Parker and his Indian war-party
Would visit the Walls and show us our fate!

For breaking the treaties the whites had all sworn to:
To keep the land free and for buffalo to roam,
The Indians had found them an easy solution,
Kill all the white settlers come to stake out their home.

Now Wayne he was sick of the sight of Fort Griffin,
And even the beauty of Mollie McCabe,
Sick to the death of the hunting and skinning,
"The Palace of Sin" had started to fade.

And, Wayne was a-drinking and cursing and shaking,
The only time steady is when he would shoot;
Then he'd sit and he'd stare at the fire all evening—
My brother had changed into some crazy coot!

So we left then behind us the Walls and Fort Griffin,
We heard of the big herds way up in the North
(For the farmers had driven their hogs to come fatten
On buffalo bodies out West of Fort Worth).

We hitched up our wagon and started up North then,
It was following the skirmish at Yellow House Draw;
We travelled at night then, all by our sweet lonesome,
And one day I found me an Indian squaw.

Her brave had done died then, and she was a widow,

She'd been left by her lone self from after the fight;
So she pitched in and helped out around the camp some,
And with crazy old Wayne, we was sure a strange sight!

For five years we wandered all over the country,
I hunted the buffalo for their thick hide;
I left their peeled bodies in devilish windrows
To poison the air in the valleys so wide.

Oh, I shot then the buffalo in hundreds of thousands,
I shipped all their hides to the dealers back East;
I trailed them and followed where they was the thickest
And after we'd finished, the buzzards would feast!

Oh, the squaw she had told me her name was Deer Running,
And sometime toward summer in our second year
(That was the year then of Eighteen-and-Eighty),
She gave me a son, a lad without peer!

Oh, Deer Running fondled and played with and rocked him,
And gave him some kind of an Indian name;
But me, I remembered how life used to be once,
And out of respect then, I named my son Wayne.

Old Wayne, when he heard that, he quit his far-looking,
And turned himself round to the problem at hand:
He picked up the baby and started to smile nice,
He dangled his watch, and pronounced the boy grand.

As for Deer Running, she didn't resent this,
She seemed like she understood and forgave Wayne,

She smiled then at all of us on the ground playing,
And turned away from us, and coughed in her pain.

At first, it did seem like her cold was a-catching,
For we all had a cough and a running nose,
But later, both Wayne's and my own, we recovered
Yet Deer Running coughed still, and was still indisposed.

Oh, Deer Running wasted from the ill of the whiteman,
Her thin body shook from the racking hard cough
Yet she cared for the baby and continued her cooking,
That was one ignorant savage whose heart was sure soft!

Oh, I took to my saddle and left the camp-fire,
I rode to the mountains the buffalo to see;
And I searched through the mountains and all the deep valleys,
But no sight of buffalo was given to me.

But there on the hillsides like the wreckage of clippers,
Like the wreckage of ships gone aground on the strand,
Were the white bones of buffalo with their ribs up a-sticking
Like the white spars of galleons thrusting up from the sand.

Oh, the wind, it did moan through the harp of their bones,
The wind it did play just a sorrowful song;
And the moon, it did light on the white scattered bones,
The moon it did shine on the buffalo—gone!

Deer Running, she told me that the buffalo ran from
The North every Spring, from deep caves in the earth;
That each year they rumbled and galloped and thundered,

Come South in their plenty with millions new-birthed.

But then in this Spring-time, though the grass was a-greening,
And the wind was a-warming, and the sky was bright blue,
We listened in vain for the sound of the buffalo,
For the time was a-passing when they surely was due!

Now a hush it had fallen all through that great country,
And no sight of a shaggy was given to us;
But just prairie flowers and a sorrowful wind then
Was all the memento of buffalo due us.

Deer Running, she told me the buffalo ran from
Deep caves in the earth from up North every Spring;
But this year no buffalo would rumble and thunder,
McLean, you poor killer, you played out your string!

At Deer Running's finish, her consumption did gallop,
And spots like red roses did blossom her cheeks;
A sweat sprang like dew on her dusk-tawny forehead,
And she choked and she coughed, but from no smoky reek!

We buried Deer Running above the blue water,
We buried Deer Running where plumberries grow;
It took us all morning to dig for her grave-place,
And before night had fallen, the bottle was low.

Now Wayne on that evening had left me all lonesome;
He did all the cooking and fed my young son—
And after he cleaned up the dishes from supper,
He sang him to sleep then before he was done.

When the boy was fast-sleeping, then Wayne came to see me,
And his eyes, they did shine with a curious glint,
And the fire, it fell on his head white as hoar-frost,
And he stammered and stuttered, a-trying to begin.

Old Wayne, he did touch me with his trembling hand;
"Say, brother," croaked Wayne, "what you do with the lad
Is leave him with me, Will, oh, leave him behind you,
I'll see to his raising, and be like a Dad.

"Oh, hell ain't half-loaded like the land of Montana,
To remind you with memories of all the bad times;
At first I could see that you hated the hunting,
The killing, the skinning, the guts and the grime.

"But you grew to love it like a duck loves the water,
And you did some fine shooting with that Sharps gun like mine—
You became a grand hunter and killer and skinner,
And being called 'Buffalo Hunter' was better than wine!

"Now the hunt takes a hold that will seldom unhand you,
Oh, the hunt takes just a remarkable hold:
It will flame in your brain, it will arise in your eyes,
It flows through your veins like the fever of gold!

"Oh, brother William, go back to your home now,
Return to dear Hartford before it's too late;
Oh, you've sported and run them, you've hunted and killed them,
The buffalo have vanished, you've shown them their fate!

"Oh, brother William, return to your home now,

60

Go back to quaint Hartford before it's too late:
There's nothing that's here in Montana to hold you,
Forget these tall mountains, and cease from your hate!

"Leave brother William, go back to your home now,
Return to old Hartford before it's too late:
But leave here your baby and brother behind you,
They're a part of your life that is now out-of-date!

"We'll bone-pick the deserts and prairies and mountains,
We'll bone-pick by sunshine and light of the moon,
We'll bone-pick with heat-stroke or teeth all a-chattering
Through chill wind of midnight or blast of the noon!

"Our world, it will shrink to the small sight before us
Of bones bleached out white on the dazzling ground—
Our backs they will cramp and our eyes they will water
As we hump along sacks full of bones that we found.

"It will seem like we've stooped down forever and ever
A-picking through graveyards of buffalo bones—
We'll search through the stands of the summers and winters
Till there's no bones of buffalo where they once roamed.

"And now they have vanished the prairie is lonely
And the welkin does ring with no shot from a Sharps
For the buffalo have gone now and with them the hunters;
No more do the winds play their bones like the harps.

"When the prairie is tidied and not even a skull now
Will escape the sore eyes of the men who bone-pick,

Then a hint of the herds will be left in the sidings
Of railroads where bones are stacked high in a rick.

"After they've vanished there remains no reminder
Left by hunters and skinners and those who bone-pick,
Of the great herds who wandered all over this country;
Why, this surfeit of slaughter should make us all sick!

"Oh, let the lad travel, I'll see to his schooling,
He'll learn to tell months from the sight of the moon,
He'll see an owl nesting and hear a coyote
And learn bloody murder does bring its own doom!

"Flee, brother William, and fly to your home now,
Bolt back to safe Hartford before it's too late!
But leave here your baby and brother behind you—
They're a part of your life which is now out-of-date!"

So, I fled to old Hartford, I returned to my home then,
I went back to old Hartford before it was late,
I strolled under elm-trees, and beheld the bright bunting,
And on the Fourth of July I did find me a mate.

Now in the winter when the moon is all shrouded
And my wife is a-sleeping so peaceful and calm,
I stand at the window, and look over roof-tops;
I pray that they both will stay safe without harm.

For over the roof-tops and steeples and gables
The snow is all settled and thicker than down,
The moon is all shrouded, the church bells all quiet,

And Hartford is safe as can be for a town.

But out on the prairie, the cold moon is blazing,
The wild wolves are howling a terrible song,
And a part of me's prowling out there on the prairie,
A part of me sings for the buffalo—gone.

Song of the Buffalo
Conclusion

• • • A<small>ND</small> thou wert plentiful!
Wide-playing as prairie grass in a summer's wind!
Wide-rolling, the thunder of thy passing
Raised the dust for as far as a young man might see!
Thick-piled as a rich brown robe flung upon the earth
Before the leaf-change of our life!
    Then pestilence stalked the prairie
                    and the desert
To strangle us with dryhacking bloodcough
And we wasted and died.
    All that was in the beginning.
    Later, it was in the single short space of
                    a young man's lifetime
Thou had departed us, left the desert, forsaken the prairie,
The mountain, the valley, the stream,
And thou wert displeased with us,
And visited us with thy absence
And we waited for thee longingly,
Keeping our faith in watching
Black bird-flutterings
In a black skull tree.

65

The Ride of "Portugee" Phillips
21-25 December 1866

THEY will tell you there were others with him too
Not just: "Phillips, John. Civilian Teamster."
Or out-of-work miner. Called "Portugee" because
He'd been born in the Azores—
That was there to make that ride from Fort Phil Kearny
To Fort Laramie with the news of the Fetterman Massacre.
It took "Portugee" four days to ride
Two hundred and thirty-six miles through driving snow;
Whoever else was with him, Dillon or Bailey or whoever,
"Portugee" Phillips left the post alone,
Rode through the raging blizzards,
And finished the final forty miles from Horse Shoe Station—
Alone.
     She tells us that before he left the post,
Phillips came to see her, wiry, bright-eyed,
Trim-bearded and gave the one-day widow of Lieutenant Grummond
His wolf-skin robe. "Here. I go because of you."
The robe, Phillips told her, was to remember him—
If Frances Grummond never saw him again.

     Lamplight pooled about the sentry post
When Colonel Carrington saw him from the fort.
Phillips was swathed in buffalo robes from head to foot,
Riding the Colonel's Kentucky Thoroughbred.
Leaned down listening to the Colonel's parting word

Trying to free his hands from the Colonel's clawlike grip.
"May God help you." Then Phillips with dispatches
Disappears from view aptly curtained
By nature's ironic artifice of falling snow.
Carrington listens for a moment then shakes his head:
"That is good, he rides the softer side of the trail."
     Tolerant, intelligent and honorable, Carrington
Mends his fast-fading footprints toward his office
Where he can in desperate measure immerse himself
With engagement of the myriad details of the cosmos
Which he had designed: Fort Phil Kearny, his world in small,
His refuge for his sundered heart:

    "Stockade of pine trunks, length 11 feet
    Tamped 3 feet in gravel & side-hewn to touching union . . "

    I came here to build, not to be beset by red barbarians;
    I am an engineer, a builder, a man of good will.
    I am surrounded by the competent, and the bloodthirsty,
    And the incompetent and loyal. It is a nightmare.

    Fetterman . . . Grummond . . . old Metzger
And his battered bugle . . . Brown . . . Jimmy's pony
Calico . . .

    ". . . a Continuous Banquette . . . Flaring Loop-Holes
For Rifles . . . BLOCK-HOUSES . . .
With Embrasures for all the Mountain Howitzers . . ."

    Loyal Captain Ten Eyck benumbed by booze
Brought me the news and then I rode past Lodge Trail Ridge:
Carnage unbelievable

69

"NOTE: Supplies . . . suitable for a peaceful civilization
Accompanied the March and Steam saw-mills followed.
Plans for buildings Eighty by Twenty-Four Feet were as follows . . ."

Phillips left alone and rode by nights
Riding south across immensities of snow-swept prairie.
His feet below the buffalo skins were bound in sacking.
His companions he left with John Friend,
The telegrapher at Horse Shoe Station.
Phillips would not delay there, for he'd promised
On his solemn word to Colonel Carrington, to bring the news
All the way to Fort Laramie, and through the drifted snow
Of Christmas Day, "Portugee" pushed on the final forty miles.
"Give me eighty men, and I'll ride knee-to-knee
through the Sioux Nation!"

You may depend upon it, you may depend upon it.
Under no circumstances will you pursue the hostiles
Past Lodge Trail Ridge. You may depend upon it . . .
Captain, Brevet Lieutenant-Colonel Fetterman had with him
A full complement of forty-nine infantry.
Grummond's cavalry added twenty-eight, and Brown,
Always spoiling for a fight, came along on Jimmy's horse;
And the two civilians: That made Eighty, and Fetterman.

I came here to build a fort, safeguard the Trail.

The sentry summoned Haas; Phillips fell
Stiffly from his frozen horse. "What is it, man?"
It was the darkness of Christmas Night, Fort Laramie,
Outside the Bachelor Officers' Quarters called "Old Bedlam"

And the temperature was showing twenty-five degrees below.
    "Portugee" Phillips stands, tottering,
Blinded by snow-glare, beard grimly decorated with icicles.
It is eleven o'clock, and the fiddles scrape.
"Portugee" Phillips stands in their midst like a huge black bear
When he brings them the news of Fetterman.

    Fetterman!

71

72

Garryowen
25 June 1876

Aн! Custer slim horseback'd gallant I'd wrest
Your secret from behind your baleful eyes, disdaining,
Full-foreboding: destined-dandy, darling
Of the warrior gods, events conspired—
You were never meant to return alive!
Seen vantag'd from above, an opera stage,
Far West chugging through tan-tumbling hills
Blue veined with cavalry; across the river
And beyond the trees,
Against the pastel morning do serenely rise
A thousand smokes in diorama skies.
Vexed, a sigh, fierce moustaches chewing.
Did you think there was little left to win,
Yet know that forward was the only open way?
Why, you dared, and dared again, and went on daring!
But live past noon-tide, and the flesh betrays:
Bad teeth, receding chin, eyes weakening, the thinning
Of those thick gold curls that would have been a woman's joy.
To these accoutrements of age you'd give scant welcome,
Your stars would long be tarnished then.
      And now the painted pennon stands out flat,
Now the terror'd sweat, neck fear prickling,
Spur sidling and rollback'd white of eye.
Farewell the message with Martini, the writing bold,
Ambiguous, in haste: ''. . . Be quick . . . Bring pacs . . .''

Gauntleted hand flung high and touching hatbrim
Above blue-quarrel'd gaze. Forward!
Blue and golden cavalry are dancing in the heated sky
And Custer to commemorate this ancient day
Shall steep the earth, dearly, with red rain
Before the failing sunlight falling, stripes the valley
With longest ray. Men follow.
Grass-scents rich from bruising hoofstrike rise.
Now echo brazen note from bugle bright-
Echoed bugle notes. Return, *trot*, to echo, *ho!*
Echo . . . echo . . . *gallop* . . . echo . . . *ho!*
Charge! And the waving wheatgrass, plumtrees bend and bow
And throw back thunder from the hills.
Spur-sound, bridle's curb chain chinks
Saddle-creak and squeal of carbine swivel-link!
Wind-rip't Custer's pennon's silk!
Wind-torn-lorn bright bugle note!
    Riding up the long last desperate dangerous ridge;
Then like divers slowly rise through blue-crystal'd water
And ascend, lungs a-bursting, to the halo'd light
And high up there amid sundazzled mist
All is suddenly clear . . . effortless.

Garryowen in glory!

from a Wm. Dinwiddie
Photograph

76

Jack Wilson's Scars

SITTING BULL sent for Kicking Bear.

Sitting Bull, he of the Hunkpapa Sioux,
He who had travelled with Buffalo Bill
Mouthing hatred unintelligible to crowds who pushed
Nickles and dimes due to the killer of Custer,
He who'd returned to Standing Rock
And in spite of attempts to unseat him
Remained the most feared and respected of Indian chiefs,
Who had a horse given him by Buffalo Bill,
Trained to lift a hoof high and paw in the air
Whenever he heard a rifle shot there.

Sitting Bull had heard it said that a new Messiah lived
Over the Shining Mountains, far away, and that Kicking Bear,
Minneconjou Sioux, had by railway car travelled to
see him there.

They had been met by two Paiutes, and then
Four days to the edge of the lake
Where they waited with hundreds more,
And shared the meal of fishes.
Finally, so Kicking Bear told Sitting Bull,
On the evening of the third day,
The Messiah had come,
Had shown them then
How to dance the dance of ghosts

That would bring back the buffalo,
Would make the brown grass green again,
Fill the dry stream-beds with bright water
And would return to them each dead hero
And for the Sioux: kill all the whites!

Take back the dance with you, Wovoka said,
Dance the dance of ghosts!

And pretty soon from the Rosebud to Pine Ridge Agency,
They danced the Ghost Dance!

Just keep an eye on it, that's all you do,
Told Lieutenant Scott at Sill to I-see-o,
It's better by far than any Philadelphia teaching
Come out West. Except for how the Sioux are taking it.

Oh-hay, oh-hay, they'd shouted at Fort Sill,
When the missionary (whose name was Gassaway)
Had tried to teach them the prayer of the Lord:
"Give us this day our daily bread,"
And all the Indians then got up, shuffled about
And agreed in loud voices, "Oh-hay! Oh-hay!"

  Ahpeatone, the nephew of old Lone Wolf, had lost a little son;
He, too, had made a pilgrimage to Wovoka,
The Indian Messiah, at Walker Lake.
Ahpeatone was disappointed, too.

  For Jack Wilson, Wovoka, the Paiute Messiah,
Dressed in store clothes lay with his face to the wall:

80

The buffalo would not return,
The brown grass never green again,
Ahpeatone never see his little son again,
The whites never go away:
Jack Wilson wanted to die.

Ahpeatone looked at Wovoka close,
And was heavy in his heart. He knew
Wovoka was not the new Messiah, for he had only
One wrist scarred, and a scar on his face.

Wounded Knee
29 December 1890

Six of the troop commanders had served
In the Seventh since Custer's time; of these,
Only one, Nowlan, had not been at the Little Big Horn.
Captain Allyn Capron commanded the artillery battery.
In the bitter wind, the lining of his coat showed red.
Then Yellow Hand had thrown up a handful of dust,
And Indians and soldiers fought face-to-face.
Capron saw at once you couldn't employ artillery
Until the soldiers disengaged.
The soldiers pulled back, leaving women, children,
Bucks, all together, all fighting.
"Nits make lice," Chivington had said to his Colorado
Volunteers at Sand Creek.

Full many a name our banners bore
Of former deeds of daring . . .

They'd dug in the trails of the four Hotchkiss
Mountain rifles, cut fuses, depressed the tubes;
Gunners had hold the lanyards. Direct fire
Into the council square, each piece throwing
A two-pound projectile, rate of fire with decent gun crew
About fifty rounds a minute. Fish in a barrel,
But they'd buck the trails in the rocky soil,
And you'd have to relay the pieces properly.
Capron was watching.

83

. . . But they were of the days of yore,
In which we had no sharing . . .

But for raw soldiers, they were doing well.
When the savages broke for the ravine,
It was too wide a swing to traverse,
And they had to shift the trails.
Two pieces fired into the camp, shifting again,
And there was nothing left alive.
One cannoneer rolled the piece right up the ravine
Firing point-blank.

. . . But now our laurels freshly won
With the old ones shall entwin'd be . . .

Afterward, when the red bastard hid in the Sibley,
We laid two rounds right in the tent with him.
He was dead then, all right. Then we finished up the ravine.

. . . Still worthy of our sires each son,
Sweet girl I left behind me.

85

Sergeant Frederick Wyllyams:
Epitaph for an Old Etonian

Fort Sam Houston, 1959.

"Unknown Indian"
"Unknown Indian"
"Unknown Indian"

F<small>ROM</small> my time at Fort Sill, this refrain
Remembered now, was reeling in my brain.

I walked through the spring sunshine of the green quadrangle
With the peacocks and pet deer.

I came to the Office of the Deputy Commanding General,
Fourth United States Army, and reported.

"Here," said the Major, pushing the large envelope
Toward me. "They hand-carried it from Sill."

Frederick Wyllyams lay face up,
Close to the camera manned
That day on the Kansas prairie.
I'd thought to see, when I'd written the Curator at Sill
For the picture I'd heard about,
Smoke in the distance, an overturned wagon perhaps,
And a huddle of bodies on the ground.

But Frederick Wyllyams lay face up,
Naked, with palms pressing down.

"Looks," said the Major, "like they used goddamned
Near everything on him. Look here, you see, bullet holes,
And there, that's where they used an axe, or hatchet,
Or something like that, next to where that spear's sticking out.
And those long cuts, there on his thighs, that's so that
He couldn't go chasing them in the hereinafter.

"Left his privates alone, anyway, and his eyes
Are still in his head. Wonder who he was?"

The Major turned over the picture.

"What the hell you want with this, anyway?"
The Major asked, suddenly sore.

I started to answer.

"Saw enough of this in the war," the Major said,
Furious with himself, his eyes welling with tears.
He looked around the office, the general gone,
Playing golf for the afternoon. The major looked
At the two captains.

"Am I right? Goddamnit, am I right?"

The Major was West Point, and had a paralysed child,
And a "compassionate" assignment to where she could learn
To crawl better, somehow, here at Fort Sam.

87

The Major waited, furiously, for me to speak.

I remembered moonlight and the willows bending:

>   "Unknown Indian"
>   "Unknown Indian"
>   "Unknown Indian"

(In West Texas, somebody's grand-mother
Used to shoo them off her porch with a broom
When they'd come begging. "Huh," she said,
"Red niggers was all they were.")

Cold moonlight and bending willows,
Red stone cairn with an eagle on the top
And I was drinking cognac.

The Major still stared at the back of the photograph.

"It is Wyllyams—he must have been Welsh."

White male, naked, bearded, well-nourished laying along
The windy sod, long cavalryman's legs disposed
Lankly, with deep bloodless gashes across the thighs;
Now he would never run through Paradise.

Wovoka, Messiah, old man, are you with us still?
Can we hear past the wind, do we have the will?

88

89

Afterword

These poems derive from my personal reactions to certain scenes of American western history and the American Indian. They are not meant to form a whole; the events they speak of are episodic, and there is no logical explanation why certain of them should receive more—or less—attention than others. They have this in common: that each story, as it influenced me, seemed to me to be unique, even if it was one that had been told many times before ("On the Fort Richardson Road," "Jack Wilson's Scars," "The Trail of Tears"), or one which, to my knowledge, had received little attention in recent times ("Sergeant Frederick Wyllyams: Epitaph for an Old Etonian").

In addition to being unrelated, many of these poems are simply personal reminiscence, and the concern with the Indian, never at less than one remove except in one or two instances, fades almost altogether from consideration.

The period of history covered by *The Promise Kept* dates from the Trail of Tears in 1838, in which Indians of the Civilized Tribes were "removed" from their homelands and forced to settle in the barren wastes of what is now Western Arkansas and Oklahoma. The poems end chronologically with the tragedy of Wounded Knee; the poems finish by the death of an Englishman serving in the Seventh Cavalry, far from the swans at Windsor. This time period comprehends the years of the great buffalo hunts, the Sioux uprisings, and the Ghost Dance.

About the Ghost Dance: Jack Wilson, the Paiute Messiah known as Wovoka, did, in fact live and preach his gospel of non-violence and trance-inducing dancing near Mason Lake, Nevada. His teachings, so patently Christian, were adopted eagerly by his pathetic following and taken back by disciples to the various reservations where the Ghost Dance was prac-

ticed. The Ghost Dance came at the end of a century which had seen the Indian culture almost completely deracinated, and its belief that the white man would, when the millennium came, disappear, must have preyed upon the minds of many of the semi-literate superstitious whites living on the frontier, and this might in some measure account for the ferocity with which the gentle movement was opposed.

The beguiling commingling of the Christian and the Indian theologies, present in the Ghost Dance teachings, is discussed by Nye at some length. The missionaries present on many of the reservations were of good Protestant stock; only in South America where the Jesuits brought about Indian conversion (largely, one supposes, by following the Roman custom of adopting elements of pagan ritual into the Christian liturgy), did the native population show an *increase* over those years.

If the Jesuits adopted Indian elements into the Roman Catholic Calendar, it might be very tentatively advanced that the Plains Indians underscored the similarity (keeping in mind that the Christian calendar itself had derived from pagan and heathen customs in dividing the year as to agricultural or hunting economies) between the Christian Church and their own important days. Of the battles initiated by the Indians, it is interesting to note which ones fell on or near dates of religious significance throughout history: the Fetterman Massacre, 21 December 1866, the Christmas season founded upon the ancient Giuli, which is itself the time of the winter solstice; Wounded Knee, 29 December 1890, close to the Feast of the Holy Innocents, a chilling irony!; The Reynolds-Crazy Horse fight, 17 March 1876, close to the vernal equinox; the Battle of the Little Big Horn, 25 June 1876, the Feast of St. John the Baptist, the time of the summer solstice. These are, of course, selected examples only. Of course, all primitive peoples may be expected to be very much aware of the changing seasons and to some extent govern their lives by them. The Comanches, attuned to the lunar calendar, planned their raids for spring and early summer, with the spring grass and a full "Comanche" moon.

Elizabeth Custer died, in New York, in 1933, only a year after Wovoka died, the prophet whose teachings triggered the tragedy at Wounded Knee. Mrs. Custer defended her husband through her long life and would listen to no detractors; as a result, there was very little of a critical nature published about General Custer until after his wife's death. Colonel Carrington, after his retirement, devoted the remaining forty-odd years of his life to defending his conduct of the Bozeman Trail forts in 1866, that dark, cold fateful year when all occasions did inform against him. In 1887, after heroic efforts, he persuaded the Senate to publish the hitherto secret reports and transcripts of the Sanborn investigation. This, Carrington felt, largely vindicated his actions. Ranald Slidell Mackenzie, superb cavalry officer, impatient, hard-driving, irritable from his wounds (Indians called him "Three Finger"), enjoyed his star as brigadier general for only two years before retiring with disability, and dying insane.

Notes

I have but scant tolerance for poetry which depends for its enjoyment upon the possession of special knowledge and rather less for poets who append a system of notes to the body of their work for enlightenment of the literary peasantry. Nevertheless, where so much of the subject of a poem is placed in the historical past, a mechanism such as these "Notes" may serve to help the reader.

The Fort Sill Officers' Open Mess

Fort Sill, Oklahoma, was originally established as an Army post in what was then Indian Territory. For over fifty years, Fort Sill has been "home" to Artillerymen.

Song of the Officers' Wives

I am being too hard on the officers' wives here. These gallant ladies for the most part bore their lot with silence and dignity.

dog-robbers . . . These were enlisted men assigned on a part-time basis, to the households of some field-grade officers.

target-cloth curtains . . . Target-cloth is the heavy, burlap-like cloth used on small-arms ranges. Often it could be claimed in almost undamaged state.

Reduction in Forces . . . This was a policy which relegated many Reserve Officers to their Regular Army non-commissioned ranks. It was not uncommon to hear of captains and majors who were reduced to their Regular ranks of corporal or sergeant.

The Echoes Are Starting

The Tenth United States Cavalry was composed of black troopers.

Colonel Benjamin H. Grierson (of Civil War "Grierson's Raid" fame) served as the commanding officer of the Tenth Cavalry from 1866–1890. The Tenth adopted the buffalo as their regimental insignia.

Geronimo's Grave, East Firing Range

Most of the Indians buried here died from smallpox.

They'll show you his cell . . . Nye says (page 386) that Geronimo spent very little time here, except on those occasions when he used it to recuperate from a crashing hangover.

"'O, Fortune!' . . ." The motto of the Artillery School is *Cedat Fortuna Peritis* which can be translated as, "Let fortune yield to experience."

The Wichita Mountain Wildlife Refuge

A handsome young couple we knew had a ranch in what seemed like the center of the Refuge. We saw them often at various social formations at Fort Sill and Lawton, and I often wondered what it would have been like to drive back through the Refuge late in the autumn, or on wild spring nights with a Comanche moon overhead.

three-dismal-two . . . In those days, 3.2 beer was the maximum strength of beer allowed to be sold in Oklahoma

Blue Beaver. A notorious tavern in the French phrase, "authentic."

"line of duty" . . . Only those injuries which came about in the "line of duty" were supposed to be billed to the government.

The Translation of Quanah Parker

Cynthia Ann Parker was taken captive by Comanche Indians in May of 1836. Quanah Parker, the child of her union with Peta Nocona, became the legendary "Eagle of the Comanches." Quanah was leader of the war party that attacked Adobe Walls on 27 June 1874. His mother was rescued by Texas Rangers in 1860, and died soon after being returned to the "white" Parker family.

Headquarters, Fort Sill, Indian Territory

The events of 27 May 1871, and following on 8 June 1871 ("On the Fort Richardson Road"), are related in Nye (pages 175–189); Utley (*Frontier Regulars*, pages 209–10), Brown (pages 244–6) and Leckie (pages 149–53).

Grierson and I could understand a man like that. Grierson was not a Regular Army Officer, but a political appointee who had been a music teacher in civilian life; Sherman, before coming back into the Army, had failed, both as a banker and as a lawyer.

"... 'City of Refuge' ... " This was what Texans called Fort Sill, since Indians under protection of the military above the Red River would make lightning raids down into Texas, and then return to their sanctuary in the environs of Fort Sill.

... "expecting every instant" ... These are Thurston's own words, as given by Nye.

The Trail of Tears

No less an authentic frontier hero than President Andrew Jackson oversaw Indian removal established as a national policy, with the enactment of the Indian Removal Bill of 1830. White settlers emigrating to what are now the central and southern United States in the early years of the nineteenth century had been severely inconvenienced to find that Indians had inhabited these parts for countless decades. Treaties had been of little real legal benefit; the sporadic attempts by Congress to aim specific legislation at the problem had been of too desultory a nature to ensure success. Indian removal, which was to evict over a ten-year period 60,000 Indians from their homelands in North Carolina, Georgia, Alabama, Florida, Mississippi and Tennessee, was a final solution to the Indian problem.

Many of the dispossessed tribes had schools, local governments, printing presses and newspapers; they built roads; enjoyed flourishing commerce not only with American merchants, but abroad, as well; some of them sent their children away to college. Many of them became missionaries.

"... inadequate preparation by the government and the appointment of a horde of political incompetents to posts of authority, resulted in woeful mismanagement and cruel and unnecessary suffering by the emigrants ... A conspicuous saving grace of this sorrowful story is the fidelity and skill with which the regular army officers and soldiers in the field discharged their unwelcome duties in connection with the removal." *Indian Removal*, page 15

The Reverend Jesse Bushyhead

"... On Tuesday evening we fell in with a detachment of the poor Cherokee Indians ... about eleven hundred Indians—sixty waggons—six hundred horses, and perhaps forty pairs of oxen. We found them in the forest camped for the night by the road side ... under a severe fall of rain accompanied by heavy wind. With their canvas for a shield from the inclemency of the weather, and the cold wet ground for a resting place, after the fatigue of the day, they spent the night. The sick and feeble were carried in waggons ... even aged females, apparently nearly ready to drop into the grave, were travelling with heavy burdens attached to their backs —on the sometimes frozen ground, and sometimes muddy streets, with no covering for the feet ... We learned from the inhabitants on the road where the Indians passed, that they buried fourteen or fifteen at every stopping place ...

"Mr. Bushyhead, ... is a very intelligent and interesting Baptist clergyman. Some of the Cherokees are wealthy and travel in style. One lady passed on in her hack in company with her husband, apparently with as much refinement and equipage as any of the mothers of New England; and she was a mother too and her youngest child about three years old was sick in her arms and all she could do was to make it comfortable as circumstances would permit ... she could only carry her dying child in her arms a few miles farther, and then she must stop in a stranger land, and consign her much loved babe to the cold ground. ..."

"When I read in the President's Message that he was happy to inform the Senate that the Cherokee were peaceably and without reluctance removed—and remember that it was on the third day of December when not one of the detachments had made even half their journey when he made that declaration, I thought I wished the President could have been there that very day in Kentucky with myself ..."

95

("A Native of Maine, traveling in the West Country" in *New York Observer*, January 26, 1839, page 4. Quoted by Grant Foreman in *Indian Removal*, pp. 305–7)

Song of the Buffalo (I & II); The Ballad of a Buffalo Hunter, William H. McLean

Few chapters of American history can be so awful as the wholesale slaughter of the great natural resource of the buffalo. From a herd once numbered from 65 to 75 millions before 1500, there were 800 buffalo left alive in 1895, most of them in private hands, and the wild ones were hunted down until less than twenty survived.

There have been many fine novels written about this period of the American West, but few, I think, are the equal of the mighty *The Last Hunt*, by Milton Lott.

The Ride of Portugee Phillips

This is one of the great rides of history.

. . . *Fetterman Massacre.* On the dark and bleak 21st of December 1866, Captain William J. Fetterman with a force of eighty men was massacred approximately four miles north-east of Fort Phil Kearny, just north of what is now Buffalo, Wyoming. Fetterman, a young officer with Civil War combat experience, had apparently disobeyed the orders given to him by his commanding officer, Colonel Henry B. Carrington, who had instructed Fetterman particularly *not to pursue* the Indians which he was being sent out to disperse from their attack of a wood-cutting party, *under any circumstances past Lodge Trail Ridge.* Captain Fetterman, who had often boasted that he would ride knee-to-knee through the Sioux nation if he were given eighty men, found himself with the required number and proceeded to disobey Colonel Carrington's explicit instructions.

. . . *widow of Lieutenant Grummond.* Frances Grummond, the young widow of the cavalry commander who died with Fetterman, later married Colonel Carrington. Phillips, not of the military, received no official recognition for his heroic ride.

"May God help you." The events at the sentry post are related by Dee Brown in his excellent book about Fort Phil Kearny.

world in small . . . Colonel Carrington, although lacking in dash and leadership, was a decent, honorable officer who was also an extremely competent engineer. Carrington's drawings of Fort Phil Kearny, the post which he was sent to build in 1866, show that it was to be a model of what a military post should be. The Sioux, however, did not give Colonel Carrington much time in which to complete his grand designs and the incessant torment of their raids, the growing insolence of his officers, the inexperience of his raw troops, the lack of arms and ammunition, all further loosened Carrington's hold. The comments pertaining to the construction of Fort Phil Kearny are taken from the sketches reproduced in Brady. Michael Straight's novel *Carrington* is a superb account of the short days of Fort Phil Kearny.

Garryowen

I find it infinitely troubling to deal at all objectively with the few minutes after noon on Sunday, 25 June 1876, when Lieutenant Colonel George Armstrong Custer and five troops of the Seventh United States Cavalry rode to death and immortality.

What remains of the Little Big Horn is that it was so perfectly complementary of the time in which it took place—it was, in its own way, operatic: Custer, the boy general, riding out to the tune of "Garryowen," Libby offstage at home at Fort Lincoln, the *Far West* chugging up a river, the flamboyant Indian scouts and even the last view we have of Custer is from the trumpeter Giovanni Martini, *alias* John Martin, who is complete with comic-opera moustaches. Nothing less would have so suited the terrain, and the enemy. What mingled terror and admiration was engendered in the Victorian breast by these simple savages and children of nature!

"Garryowen" is the eighteenth-century Irish tune that the Seventh Cavalry adopted as its regimental song.

Blue and golden cavalry are dancing . . . In *Boots and Saddles*, Elizabeth Bacon Custer describes the mirage which was her last view of her husband and of the Seventh Cavalry as they left Fort Abraham Lincoln, near Bismarck, North Dakota.

effortless . . . Of course it was not effortless. But by then, the participants were locked into conflict which had only one resolution.

Jack Wilson's Scars

Those who prayed, taught Wovoka, and those who danced the Ghost Dance, and who wore the magical ghost shirts, and sang the songs, would "die" and be allowed brief glimpses of their dear dead friends and relatives. However, they must not hurt anyone. The outcome of the Ghost Dance, of course, was the reappearance of the buffalo, and game, and the absence of all whites. The Sioux, who had recently suffered severe set-backs at the hands of "civilization" were particularly receptive to the perverted version of what Wovoka taught: that the millennium he prophesied could be accelerated by killing *all* the whites.

This story, particularly in relation to the Sioux, is told fully in Utley's *Last Days of the Sioux Nation*.

Wounded Knee

More than 150 Indians were killed at Wounded Knee during the events of 29 December 1890. Twenty-five officers and soldiers were killed, and 39 wounded. At least sixty-two of the dead were women and children.

Sergeant Frederick Wyllyams: Epitaph for an Old Etonian

This photograph which I have in my possession, is from the collection of the U.S. Army Artillery and Missile Center Museum, Fort Sill, Oklahoma. On the reverse side, there is the following note:

"Sgt. Frederick Wyllyams, Co. "G", Seventh Cavalry, killed near Fort Wallace, Kansas, by Cheyennes 25 June 1867. Wyllyams was an Englishman of good family, a graduate of Eton, and at the time of his death was in daily expectation of a commission in the U.S. Army, having passed his examination . . ."

Wyllyams was killed, it appears, nine years to the day before his regiment, the Seventh Cavalry, lost five troops at the Little Big Horn; a reconstituted Seventh was also present at Wounded Knee, in 1890.

Selected Bibliography

Brady, Cyrus Townsend. *Indian Fights and Fighters* (New York, 1904. Reprint, Lincoln, 1971).

Brown, Dee. *Bury My Heart At Wounded Knee: An Indian History of the American West* (New York, 1971).

———. *Fort Phil Kearny, An American Saga* (New York, 1962).

Dary, David A. *The Buffalo Book* (Chicago, 1974).

Fehrenbach, T. R. *Comanches. The Destruction of A People* (New York, 1974).

Foreman, Grant. *Indian Removal* (Norman, 1932).

Gard, Wayne. *The Great Buffalo Hunt* (Lincoln, 1959).

Leckie, William H. *The Military Conquest of the South Plains* (Norman, 1963).

Lott, Milton. *The Last Hunt* (Boston, 1954). Novel.

Mooney, James. *The Ghost Dance Religion and the Sioux Outbreak of 1890*, 14th Annual Report of the Bureau of American Ethnology. (Washington, D.C. 1896).

Neihardt, John G. *The Twilight of the Sioux* (Lincoln, 1971). This contains "The Song of the Indian Wars," and "The Song of the Messiah" which comprise Volume Two of Neihardt's beautiful poetry of *A Cycle of the West*.

Nye, Captain, W. S. *Carbine and Lance. The Story of Old Fort Sill* (Norman, 1937).

Sheridan, Lieutenant General Philip Henry. *Outline Descriptions of the Posts in the Military Division of the Missouri* (Chicago, 1876. Facsimile Edition, The Old Army Press, Fort Collins, Colo., 1972).

———. *Record of Engagements With Hostile Indians Within the Military Division of the Missouri, 1868–1882* (Washington, 1882. Facsimile Edition, The Old Army Press, Fort Collins, Colo., 1972).

Straight, Michael. *Carrington* (New York, 1960). Superb novel.

Utley, Robert M. *Frontier Regulars. The United States Army and the Indian 1866–1890* (New York, 1973).

———. *Last Days of the Sioux Nation* (New Haven, 1963).

Vaughn, J. W. *Indian Fights. New Facts on Seven Encounters* (Norman, 1966).

Type set by G & S TYPESETTERS
Printed by PRINTING CRAFT
Paper supplied by LONE STAR PAPER COMPANY
Bound by CUSTOM BOOKBINDERY
Design by WILLIAM D. WITTLIFF